www.toabutterfly.com

Thoughts of a Butterfly
© 2011 Shirley J. Ramos

ISBN: 978-1456426347

Thoughts of a Butterfly

A Journey to

Let Go . Laugh . Live . Love

Shirley J. Ramos

CONTENTS

Acknowledgments

There are many people I want to thank for helping me reach this point. I will begin with an important teacher in my life – my mother, Elena. She guided me, shaped my character, and taught me how to really love. I dedicate this book to her.

Thank you to my father, Freddy, who taught me to dream big and opened my mind to the philosophies of life. To my best friend in the world – my brother, Bryan; there are no words that can quantify my feelings for him and his family: Carmen, Tyler, Nathaniel, Amanda, and Grace. Mylene and Mario, they kept me going. To Abuelita Toña, Mama Ana, Papa Alfonso, I wouldn't be here without them. To two special souls, Diana and Andrea, who sat by my side while I wrote. To Jeffrey, a man who blessed my life, and to the countless friends and family members I've shared my life with, I thank you all. Lastly, I thank God for the butterfly that blessed my life all those years ago. The love it taught me grows daily.

Introduction

"I am sorry Shirley… you have suffered a stroke." I heard these words spoken as my twenty-nine years of life as I knew them came to an end.

However, my story did not end there.

"You were created for a purpose Shirley. Like a butterfly emerging from its chrysalis after a magical transformation, you too will emerge from this ordeal, a new creature." In the days and months to follow, these words echoed through the chambers of my heart. Ironically, it was a hole in this same heart that almost ended my life.

Since then, *Thoughts of a Butterfly* has become an instrument for understanding my own metamorphosis – one that is helping me to find my purpose, my spirit. Let Go - Laugh - Live - Love are the core values I've discovered – values I make a conscious effort to live by.

This is only the beginning of the journey. Now, this book brings it all to the surface where others can take whatever helps or inspires them. Though I wrote *Thoughts of a Butterfly*, I've come to understand it's not about me.

Wholeheartedly, I thank you for your support and love.

Wake Up

He said:
You've been sleeping twenty-plus years.
Time to wake up, my child.
I need you to awaken.
You're now called to the wild.
And don't you fear,
you're not alone.
I let you sleep so long,
to prepare you for my own.

December 10, 2000

Lost

"Do not now seek the answers, which cannot be given you because you would not be able to live them. And the point is, to live everything. Live the questions now."
~Rainer Maria Rilke

Life in my twenties was a series of events that would make for an interesting anthropological study, with the final analysis resulting in a resounding, "This girl is lost!"

What didn't I try? What avenue didn't I explore to enable growth in life? I was a student, a hairdresser, a bartender, a waitress, an office assistant for a buyer, a party planner, a party promoter – and by the time I was twenty-three, I had changed directions yet again, becoming a mortgage banker. I was following big dreams of being super-successful… whatever that meant.

Don't ask me how it all worked out; it kind of just did. God had a sense of humor and He blessed me with serendipity. I met interesting people and made the best out of most situations, but I lacked direction and had no idea what I really wanted, or how to get it. However, was I really any different from others in their twenties?

By the summer of 2008, at the ripe age of twenty-nine, I had experienced some extensive heartbreaks in my relationships; on an intimate basis, friendship, and professionally. I wondered what I was doing with my life. I desperately sought some kind of order and focus, but was not able to achieve it. Some elements in my life had left me feeling hopeless, and I needed a goal to know there was purpose to my existence. "I can do this," rang in my head, though I couldn't define what "this" really meant.

True to my 'think big' form, the NYC Marathon came up on my radar. I figured with four months to train, what is twenty-six point two miles? I can do it, and how amazing would it be to run in the city I was born in, the city that claims my soul? Fortunately, I was chosen as a runner for a prominent charity and had to raise money for this worthy cause, so I finally had a purpose, a tangible goal other than serving my own desires.

The day after I was chosen to run, as fate would have it, I was rear-ended. I could have taken this as an omen to quit, but instead I chose to go through with physical therapy and began training a few weeks later. I was determined to accomplish my goal.

The NYC Marathon happened to coincide with Halloween, and I couldn't resist the urge to party on Friday night. After all, who throws a Halloween party quite like NYC? My hope was to be well enough to wake up at four a.m. Sunday to run.

For Halloween, I dressed up as a police officer and when I arrived at the party, I realized I'd forgotten my handcuffs. Feeling a bit disappointed, I made it a mission to locate handcuffs at this party. Ten minutes into the fiesta, I saw another police officer costume, and the wearer happened to have two pairs of handcuffs hanging from his belt. This was the sign I needed to start a conversation.

This brilliant and wise man not only gave me a set of handcuffs, but he also shared his wisdom about running the NYC marathon, as he had done it five times. He mentally prepped me about what to expect. He spoke of running across the Queensboro Bridge, and how that moment would be extremely emotional.

It was a great evening. Seeing my friends have such a good time and sharing an inspirational conversation left me feeling full of energy and ready to run the marathon. The morning of the race, I felt a range of emotions: Fear, joy, nervousness, appreciation, love, and gratitude. You name it – I covered the emotional spectrum that day. True to the wise man's counsel, I was emotional when I crossed the Queensboro Bridge. As I heard the roars of the crowds on First Avenue, my emotions were triggered again. Then, at mile eighteen, I saw my family: my past, and my present colliding into my future, into my reason for being. That moment, I felt running for a cause was the right thing to do. It was an amazing experience – one that changed my life.

After returning home from this moving experience – and regaining the use of my legs – reality seeped in and doubts crowded my thoughts. I was not where I wanted to be. I was still heartbroken, confused, and hopeless. The past year seemed like a calamity of failures. In stark contrast to the success of completing the NYC Marathon, the rest of my life was running in the wrong direction. My brief move to NYC failed due to the economy; my relationships with men failed; my career in an industry that was greatly responsible for the world's financial collapse highlighted my dismay, and I didn't have any real prospects of what I wanted to do. This in addition to all the debt I had managed to get myself in and

4

the stresses tied to those disasters… I was a mess without a purpose!

Although I had numerous problems, the one that carried the most weight was not having a special person in my life, someone to love me for me, to buoy me through the rough seas of my own creation. I had been in a series of relationships that had left my spirit broken. There were lessons learned, but sometimes I had to repeat them. It wasn't fun to keep hitting myself against the same wall and not understand why I was being exposed to such drama. There were major holes in my intimate relationships, but there was something in me that could not let go of the quest for the intimate bond I longed for, and felt I deserved. The relationships I continued to engage in lived far beyond their expiration dates. I was ready for it all to stop. But how?

The power to make the failures end was within me; I just didn't know it. I continued to make mistakes for a while longer… until it happened. I experienced a night that undoubtedly changed my life.

The following thoughts are a glimpse into my lost mind. A place I desperately sought to find my way out of...

Losing Myself

Here I am again lost amongst words,
lost in thought, lost in life.
I have managed to condemn my soul,
to this lonely cell, with only a little ray of light.
I have allowed the love I once felt,
the hopes and dreams I created,
to sentence me to a place without decisions…
in fear of being hurt again.

And what I find most challenging,
I see, I know, and I'm scared.
Aware of the culprit,
yet still I stay here, stay and ponder.
How did the failures of past loves
break my spirit so much that
I feel I'm sunk into quicksand?

God, I know I need to let go,
but I have come to crossroads
of choices, and decisions of the past...
hope in every decision I've made.
That hope, that feeling of thinking I'll be fine,
is the very challenge which has me currently crippled.

If I go left, I can expect ABC.
If I go right, I can expect XYZ.
So which one is it?
The beginning or the end?
Or is the end the beginning?
Where is this journey taking me?
And more importantly, is my heart healed enough
to endure the pains that balance the joys of life?
How long do I sit here quietly?
How long do I wait; where is the magical sign?
The sign which blessed my life in the past.
I will continue to pray,
and hopefully achieve the clarity
I desire, long for, and need.
I want to fulfill my purpose.
I want to become who God intends me to be.
I just need a little time out in life…
I need to reflect, regroup,
and embrace the life with which I am blessed.

Broken

As I lay here late at night
with only the thoughts of my mind,
I can't resist looking back
and wonder, am I where I'm supposed to be?
I have been a good person,
but I'm aware of my impulsive decisions.
Could the circumstances of my past,
the desperate desire to do things right
(wrapped in poor choices),
could these events create a broken soul?

My mind is consumed with these thoughts,
opposite concepts such as heaven and hell.
I will not succumb to despair.
Though there are moments when
I don't know what else to feel.
An endless weight on my chest,
tears start swamping, drowning my eyes,
as if the liquid, too, needs to escape from within my head.
I hold them in.
If I release them, they become real.
I will have no choice, but to look at their depths,
and accept that my decisiveness created them.

Can I handle this cruel truth?
How did I get here?
It all happened so fast.
In a blink of an eye, my soul – penetrated.
But by what?

God, I know you are there –
you must feel the torture I endure.
How can someone full of positivity,
write such dramatic, depressing words?

It's dawn and I wonder… am I broken?
The loneliness of night accompanies me.
I look in the mirror and wonder if my reflection
will be the only sight I have during this internal war.
Will there be someone who understands and accepts,
this mind full of dark thoughts?
Why do I feel the need to connect with another soul –
can't I escape alone?

All I can hear in my mind is broken…broken…broken.
Please… fix it.

Walking to Temptation

There is a look to you...
You trigger the curiosity in my mind,
the curiosity that wants to know you a little better.
I have known of you for years,
yet never had the eyes I have for you now.

You intrigue me.
Your allure captures my thoughts and it's scary.
I know you and your capabilities,
and feel daring enough to enter your world.
I think once you taste my essence,
you will want me as I want you.

You are a challenge...
This desire and want, so strong.
It may not be good, but the magnetic force,
keeps reeling me in.

What will I learn in this journey and
are you worth the pain I may experience?
Can I keep my strength,
and all that makes me a woman,
intact while holding you here with me?

I fear you, but want you.
Two feelings, opposing philosophies.
Dangerous and exciting.
The energy captivates me.
You torment me.
This experience sentences my soul.
As good as I may feel at times,
will it be at the expense of my spirit?

I still choose to jump in...
though I know the destiny that awaits me.
May God protect me on this high.

Thoughts in the Dark

When I look back
and think of all the hurt you caused me,
my body flinches
at the pain you exposed me to.
I will never understand *why* you did what you did.
Your actions, so callous… calculated.
You knew my next step before I did,
using it to your advantage.
I was bogged in the mire that I thought was "love."
But there was no love there,
only a web of lies, fear, and betrayal.
These negative elements invaded my mind,
causing me to feel lost and confused.
Some days I thought I had the strength to pull it together.
I thought I saw the light glimmering in the darkness.
As I ran to this light,
it would fade away and I would simply be tired.
Tired from running, tired from thinking,
tired of feeling stuck, so stuck.
There was a weight on my chest...
at times, I couldn't even breathe.
How did this end up being my life?
Where did I go so wrong?
I lay at night, my attention focused on the cross on the wall.
I would privately pray,
"God, I'm meant for more – this isn't the life I should live."
I would just lie there
until my eyes could no longer handle the weight of pain.
My lids would shut, and I slept.
The next day I woke wondering if I was dreaming.
Then I would look at my surroundings,
all the material *stuff* I had accumulated,
and I was faced with the reality;
this is the life I allowed to exist in my soul.

Your Negative Presence

You are here again,
to disrupt the calm my soul yearns for,
your presence attempting to captivate me.
You would like nothing more than to seize my mind,
ultimately causing me to be lonely, insecure, and sad.

You cannot win this time.
There is something stronger in me now,
that you can never touch.
Perhaps I didn't always make the best decisions.
Some opportunities never yielded fruit.
But, I will not lose sight of what I feel with certainty.
There is something special in my soul,
being unearthed through time and awareness.
The layers of the past shed away,
as I grow into the woman I am meant to be.

My vision is to share experiences with others,
to shield them from making similar mistakes.
You will never have me again; you cannot win this battle.
I feel your torture, as you steer me down memory lane,
causing me to think of past things, depressing,
while you try to stunt my growth.

I feel no pity, nor do I regret my past.
All decisions, successes and failures of the past –
I own those moments because they made me who I am today.
Though some experiences brought an ocean of tears,
I will break the shackles you've had on me.
You try to confuse me with distinct purpose,
and prevent me achieving the clarity I seek.

I am close, it's within my reach.
Very soon, I will take the leap of faith, and fly.
You might create obstacles hard to overcome,
But I cannot be stopped.

Unnecessary

Years have gone by since you were by my side.
Life has changed, we have grown in different directions.
Yet, you still hold on to what we once were.
Perspective is subjective, able to take a life of its own.
It has distorted your view of the reality we once lived.

I don't remember all those 'happy times' that live in your mind,
I can't get lost daydreaming in such a blissful past.
That is not what I encountered, not what I felt –
my heart does not recall such joy and peace.

Complications were always at our center.
Your fidelity was not clear to me.
I now know, though you may have been there physically,
you really weren't there at all.
I remember the endless tears I cried,
the silent prayers that something would change,
the hope we would finally work it out.
These wishes never were fulfilled.

Once we went our separate ways,
I was stuck in an in-between state.
The pain of not having you around
would allow me to contemplate,
"Maybe I could have done something else."
I took on the weight of our failures,
and internalized the despair I felt.

You had such a hold of me,
even in separation, you could trigger a reaction.
You would ruin my days with your words,
bring me to tears, make me doubt myself.
Thank God, those days are over now.
There is nothing inside that holds any guilt
about our time together.
I don't question why things happened,
I have no reason to be angry anymore.
I have finally let go and accepted that
our experience was a lesson I had to learn.

There is no reason to explain or justify our past.
Appreciating the life I have now,
looking forward to the dreams I will live tomorrow,
this is what fills my heart.
I don't look back or relive past dramas.
My heart sees something no one can ever take from me.
So now, to talk about the past... is simply unnecessary.

Sabotage

I knew better about certain experiences
I, nevertheless, allowed myself to live.
I entered situations already knowing the end result.
Did I have vague hope that things would be different,
or, did I sabotage any growth I attained?

Two steps forward,
God knows the tremendous efforts I made
to reach a place where my heart began healing.
And then… I stepped back,
reliving old thoughts and hopes.

Focus was not where it needed to be.
The result; feeling hurt and alone.
Once again, it was I, who sabotaged my self.
Why did I allow myself to get lost?
What lessons must I learn?
What message was not clear to me?

My heart knew where I wanted to be,
who I wanted to become,
the sacrifices needed to achieve this end.
What negative forces prevented me making strides?

Love was in my soul.
Love I wanted to share with others.
But I cannot share this with everyone.
It's sacred, private, and I cherish this gift.
I struggled with how to release the energy.
My mind, needing 'reprogramming,'
in order to analyze future outcomes.

A certain awareness to be finessed,
my center, the inner voice I so often ignored,
the missing element.

Though I Understand

It's late at night as I try to get my thoughts together.
So much can occur in so little time.
I wonder, "Why is this all happening?"

My mind has grown this year.
So many experiences, traumas, and lessons required.
I now appreciate all things
and have come to accept my place in life.
I look forward to future achievements.
The strength of my ancestors, immediate family,
the influences that shaped my being,
demands a level of responsibility to these souls.
They all sacrificed so much in their lives,
I must be strong and fulfill my purpose.

Understanding doesn't negate the hurt.
Life's lessons are complex and deep in webs
the bare eye cannot always see.

This morning I woke with nothing but thoughts of love,
so hopeful and full of energy.
And as I lay here at night,
my optimism still exists,
but anguish accompanies the hope of love.

Memories are ever present.
Conflicting beliefs coexisting in my mind,
as if there is no choice in their destiny.
There is no alternative, but to accept the life and lessons –
live and learn.

Flooded with emotions, I am speechless.
Words to describe my feelings are hard to discover.
My thoughts haven't evolved enough for me to understand.
I lay here, love, and hope...
but I also say to myself,
though I understand, it can still hurt.

Awoken

"The really important events in my life happened in spite of me.
I had no control over them."
~Isabel Allende

February 22, 2009: Something terrifying and dark was pulling me, deep in my sleep. I saw a man without a face walking toward people and placing his hand on their right shoulder, and they would quickly collapse like marionettes without their strings. My life, I sensed, was in real danger. From out of the darkness, three angels surrounded me, protecting me from the faceless man. Shuttling me indoors and out, trying to outrun this mad, faceless monster, the three angels only spoke six words, "Shirley, you need to get up!"

I could see the faceless creature at a distance, and though he did not have eyes, I felt he was focused on me. As the creature walked in my direction, my angels insisted that I needed to get up, but I repeatedly said, "I can't." Responding required all the energy I could muster. I was stuck in this black, terrifying hole. I struggled for hours trying to wake from this deadly sleep.

My angels had protected me thus far, but as the dark force came closer, I knew I had to do something to help myself. At this point (in what I hoped was a just a dream), I was outside and everything was black. There was a red roller coaster in the background, and my angels hid me behind the single green bush. They said again, "YOU NEED TO GET UP!"

While in this terrifying dream, I heard a phone ringing. I wasn't sure what was real: the ringing, or the monster. The ringing seeped into my sleep, and the sound was the wake-up call I desperately needed.

I jolted up and faced the mirror before my bed. Disoriented, I looked across the room and realized that I was experiencing double vision in my left eye. It was a strange sensation and the objects around me felt extremely unnatural. Caller ID had registered the missed call. The call that would prove to have saved my life was from my mother.

Minutes later, the phone rang again. My mother's somewhat panicked voice came through the line. "Where have you been? We've been calling you all morning. How could you sleep so late?"

"I don't know, I feel really weird," my speech was different and slurred. I knew something peculiar was going on, but didn't know exactly what it was. I asked her, "What time is it, where am I... what day is it?" The confusion, the double vision, the remnants of the dream overwhelmed me.

She answered, "Two p.m." Two p.m.? I looked at the clock. Two p.m. I had been asleep since midnight the night before. Fourteen hours? I was supposed to be at my brother's house, celebrating his birthday with my family. It was very unlike me to sleep so long and to miss a family occasion.

I stumbled out of bed and immediately fell to my right side. My balance was non-existent and I could not stand up straight. I had to lean against the wall while using my arms to pull me, and keep me on my feet. I managed to stagger to the bathroom. I looked in the mirror, and was bewildered. The eye experiencing double vision was accentuated by the collapse of that side of my face. I was terrified before, but this, this made the dream pale in comparison to my lopsided face and double vision.

In my haze, I looked at my cell phone and noticed I had a text message from my girlfriend, which read: "Hey, I saw you called me at 4:30 am... are you ok?" I didn't understand how I could have called her so early since I was asleep for so long. I had trouble operating the cell phone. The device I could hardly live without confused me now. But I managed to get her on the phone and asked if I had left a message. I had not, so I was still confused, dazed, and feeling strange. I asked her if she wanted my purses in case I died. I guess somewhere in the darkness, I grasped the gravity of my situation.

Next, I called my mother again. I struggled with the phone and couldn't even recognize numbers. I was able to use my touch screen, find the phone log, identify my mom, and tap her most recent call. The call went through, thank God.

When I got my mother on the line, I told her I didn't feel well and was going to stay home. Ironically, I was more concerned about missing my brother's birthday celebration and ruining the family's plan for lunch, rather than what was happening to me. Mom wanted to come home, but I pleaded with her not to leave my brother's home. She said she was going to call my aunt to check on me, in spite of my asking her not to bother. A parent's instinct kicked in and both my mother and father reacted. In hindsight, their intuition almost certainly saved my life.

I then called a friend because I was scared and wanted to hear a voice that made me feel safe. I mumbled and rambled about my condition and he assured me I was going to be okay. I desperately wanted to believe him. Minutes later, the doorbell rang and it was my aunt. She walked behind me into the kitchen. All I could do was hold myself against the wall to obtain a semblance of balance. My eye was hyper-sensitive to light and I felt extremely weak.

I began telling her that someone was trying to kill me in my dream. I know my conversation must have sounded strange, but death was the only thought in my mind. My aunt quickly assessed the situation, the slurred speech, the unsteady walk, the droopy face, and convinced me to let her take me to the hospital. I didn't want to go because it would only confirm my fear something was terribly wrong, and I didn't want to face that. She was steadfast and firm, yet kind in her insistence that I get in her car.

Even though I wasn't entirely lucid, I insisted on changing into cute sweat pants and a matching shirt. I felt very bad, but I didn't want to look the part too. I slowly clipped my hair half up and half down and tried to apply mascara. I was taking my time – stubborn as the sign of Aries dictates – because I wanted to prove I was still in control. I couldn't see right, I didn't feel like myself, and this was a very hard reality for me to accept.

When we arrived at the hospital, the registered nurse looked intently at me as I described my symptoms to her. She directed me to a seat in the waiting area. The sunlight streaming in the window made me blink and falter, so I shielded my eyes and clung to my aunt for support. I kept my head down to avoid both the brightness, and the reality of my situation.

A nurse called me back and assigned me to room number eight. Medical personnel took my vital signs and the doctor asked me questions about what I was experiencing. The doctor said he would like to get an MRI done and I didn't have the clarity of mind to ask questions, or to comprehend how he managed to schedule it so quickly in an emergency room.

I can still remember today the cold sensation of fear as the tech rolled my bed into the MRI room. He strapped me down and slid me into the cylinder. As the MRI machine began to work its magic, I recall vividly dreaming wild scenes, seeing bright colors, and hearing many sounds without any idea of what I was experiencing. I felt I was somewhere not quite in this world. Then the machine stopped, the dreams ended, and I was back in the hospital. Dazed and confused, I was wheeled back into room number eight.

By this time, my aunt had called my parents and they were in my room when I returned. We were all perplexed, but couldn't, or wouldn't, imagine that my condition was anything severe or permanent. My father was very supportive, saying, "Tu estas sufriendo de estrés, pero todo va a estar bien. No te preocupes." It was comforting to hear my condition was only stress and everything was going to be okay. I wanted to believe him, but I knew he wasn't right.

Shortly after he spoke those words, the doctor walked in and said, "I am sorry Shirley, but we are going to have to admit you. You have suffered a stroke." At that second, I had a 'movie moment.' I looked at my loved ones sitting in the room with me; slowly I stared at their faces, their eyes, and then closed my own. My tears began to fall. Even in this state, I thought how odd it was that I could only feel the tears slide down the right side of my face. My mother rushed to my bedside, held my hand, and cried with me. I felt so helpless, sad, shocked, confused – it was too much to register and process all at once. All I could do was lie there with a blank expression, tears running down my face. How did this happen to me?

The following are a series of thoughts that capture my journey to awaken from the nightmare my life had become...

Confusion

Looking back at experiences,
confusion has played a recurring role
in the story of my life.

I lived through intense love affairs,
and opened the gates to my core
to some who evoked a tsunami of wounds.
They clouded my thoughts until my vision misted.

I have been lost many times over,
asking, "Why am I experiencing this?"
Still living it, because wisdom hadn't developed.

Many times, the thread of my religious influences
would drive me to madness,
as I questioned... is the devil after me?
So many thoughts, so many heartbreaks...
and confusion always at the center.

Not only did I experience it,
but the extension of my disarray
entangled others,
consistently increasing chaos.
I'd be baffled at the words of some,
and even more so, at their actions.
To trigger reactions, a feeling, anything...
it didn't matter if it were wrong or right.
The idea of having me around
would cause extreme and unhealthy behavior.
Confusion again would sit at the center of this madness.

What was interesting, with time,
confusion gained more strength.
Webs of desperation grabbed hold of me tighter,
and tighter, to the point of suffocation.
I needed to breathe, to exhale,
but even that simple task became unachievable.
I look back, I live with all the memories,
many questions racing to my mind.
I understand things happen for a reason,
but wonder if those reasons were worth calmness of spirit.

Now, I choose to live differently.
I protect my environment, my soul.
I cannot allow it to be broken again,
by bad choices.
My dreams will not be shattered at my own hands.
Heart and mind work interdependently.
One cannot live without the other, but they coexist.
It took a trauma to 'get' this, but now I understand.

There will be future struggles.
However, there is no confusion attached
to the understanding of the gift, that is my life.

On My Way

So much time has passed
since I lived in those moments,
when my early years had a hold of me.
Back then, my mind wandered.
Attempts to rescue me occurred,
yet youth enchanted me with the vapidity of arrogance.
I thought I'd be fine and didn't need anyone.
I only needed to 'explore' to find myself –
what truly made me happy.
I could no longer utilize advice from others.

Sadly, I wasn't ready.
My heart journeyed to places I couldn't have imagined.
There were times of excitement and intrigue.
Many mysteries were revealed to me.
There was no regret on my path.
My skin began to grow tough,
maturity shaping my life,
but, perspective was lost along the way.

Seeing so much, I no longer knew what I wanted.
I tried to make squares fit into circles,
I attempted to make the wrong, right.
The truth of the matter is,
I tried too hard for things that didn't,
in reality, merit my attention.

Though I was living… sadly, I wasn't ready.
Knowledge and experience, I garnered.
With all I had seen, there was no reason not to 'get it.'
But I failed to recognize experience, dressed up with cynicism,
and this element blindsided me.

This ever-so-powerful emotion
enabled my mind to live recklessly.
I thought I was strong, ready to beat the game.
So, I continued with a good heart,
but impaired by cloudy vision.

Sadly, I wasn't ready.
Waking one morning, after the worst dream of my life,
the dark of night almost became my reality.
But love found a way to grab me –
it rang so loud, it was real.
It saved my life.

I lay here now with a perspective, changed,
there is truth in all that surrounds me.
Blessed by insight and reflection,
I am guided on my way.
My heart and mind are ready… now.

Thoughts in an Office

I am utterly frustrated.
A hurricane of thoughts,
feelings, and emotions flood my brain.
What do I do next, and is this dream possible?
Is it fear that I am feeling?
Whatever it is, I don't like it.

I am not meant to be stuck here,
sitting at a desk, wondering how will I make money.
Passion, even the tiniest bit,
for my current career, is nonexistent.
The inevitable question is what do I do now?
It's been a crazy year...

Certain insights have been gained,
a perspective luckily achieved,
but how to put it all together?
Will I be able to fight off anxiety?
I hope doubt subsides as confidence rises.

Too many thoughts. I try to hold it together.
Madness, threatening to overwhelm me, will not succeed.
Fear of the unknown can't stop me.

I do admit, however, to a level of uncertainty.
"Get it together!" I tell myself.
"You cannot let your soul be tormented.
You have to fight, it is who you are!"
Repetition of these words becomes mantra.
I hope it leads to courage.

Beauty within me must radiate.
This is only a fleeting moment.
Anxiety won't last for long.
I pray this burden departs my space soon.
If it doesn't, I will embrace the obstacle
because I may not get over this situation,
but I will get through it.

Reflections

Life is not what I ever expected.
It has molded itself into both good and bad.
With all that has happened,
I have realized the key is to prepare my mind.
I am not one to shift things for only my satisfaction...
nor am I one to dictate, or say, what life should be.
I'm simply a pawn in this game of chess.
With deep concentration and focus,
a pawn can also play a strategic role.
Too much of my life,
I've tried to control situations and circumstances.
My God-given talents went misused,
adapted to my tunnel vision.
I am that person no longer.
My life, heart, and mind have shifted.
I will not let my second chance of life go to waste.
I see my light, have asked for signs…
my faith in something powerful
will guide and protect upon this journey.
All experiences were necessary for the insights
revealing themselves daily.
This is the life I choose to live.

The Mirror

As I sit here now,
looking at my former thoughts,
words, fears, confusion –
I want to reach back into the past
and take hold of that lost girl, so misguided.

I am not her anymore.
My life took the turn it needed.
I am achieving the clarity my soul desperately yearned,
and won't let go of this place... ever.

Before I was distracted, tempted
by forces more important than my being.
Emotions tied to relationships,
becoming consumed in the other person,
trying to discover why things weren't working,
were all forces stronger than my own will.
Living blissfully was something I desired,
but I didn't make consistent efforts
to exist in that state of mind.

My attempts, I thought, were enough to sustain me,
yet the cloud of confusion followed
even when I thought I had passed it by.
The grip of self-absorption was a powerful one –
especially because I didn't even see it.

My thoughts, desires, aspirations were all tied to my satisfaction.
An essential conscious balance was needed.
Now, I recognize, yes, the aspiration to be happy is a good one.
But this energy released to the universe unprotected,
can be side-swiped by other forces.

Awareness is required, and for me
this has developed with time.
Time has led me to this truth, which blossoms daily.
My reality is now searching for meaning.
I am aware my spirit guides this journey.
I now feel ready to live the life my heart truly desires.

The Voice

It's about self-doubt and uncertainty entering my life.
All positive thoughts and aspirations are there,
except now I hear a voice
telling me why I can't do certain things.
The voice is taunting, agonizing.
Its tone deceptive, creating the instability it desires.
I know this voice and its goal.
So why am I still affected by its presence?
I wonder if knowing the voice has the power to make it go away.
It is just a voice after all.

Its strong pull is undeniably present.
However, I will not succumb to the destructive appeal.
I wonder if this voice is scared of me.
It has to be, why else would it work so vigilantly
to throw me off track and discourage my vision?
But now my real voice guides my spirit.
I walk with a genuine force, untouchable.

My mind belongs to another,
and if this foolish pretender dares do battle with me,
it will lose, miserably.
I was sentenced to a lie for so many years...
and it's time for truth to prevail.
Lies can no longer occupy a room in my life.
My heart only has space for the one true voice,
the one that really belongs there.
That voice belongs to my spirit.

A Force

I feel the energy surrounding my essence.
There is a direction I need in my life and
sacrifices required to make it happen.
There is no other way, but this.
Obstacles confront me time and again.
Situations and moments with the single motive
of throwing me off course.

My heart is spiritually unimpaired –
it can no longer be touched.
Now I fight for the conviction,
to lead my mind toward its destiny.
As easy as it is to write this concept,
the actual act of alignment is not so simple.
Complications get in the way.
Even moments I aspire to, or love.

All that feels good should be right,
but even those circumstances may not be right,
for the right reasons.
At this point, I would have it no other way.
I need purpose, I yearn for meaning, and seek truth.

This force has captured my soul.
Nothing can compete with this strength.
Finally, I've given in to realizing that this silent spirit
will lead me to experiences beyond imagination.
I am ready for this part of my life.

For years, I waited for creativity and passion to be unleashed.
The clarity I carry inside is unimpeded.
I don't know what future experiences I will live,
but I am now prepared.
A force matures daily.
A vision of something great.
Fear is controllable, love is at the core.

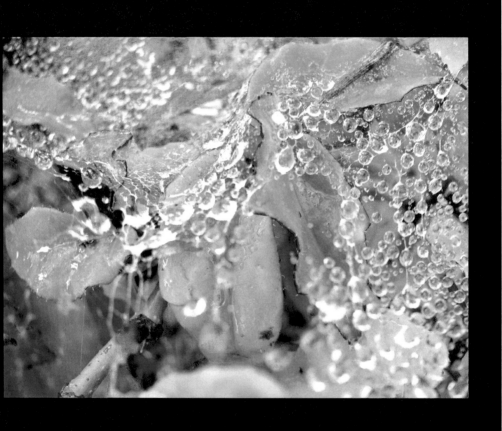

Chasing Love

How many times have I heard the words, "I love you?"
Three words that hold such meaning and power.

They have the ability to make me feel things
I would not have,
without the strength of their presence.
God knows I've wanted love more than words can express.
I needed this emotion, an unconditional connection.
Love had a way to find me, not the way I quite expected,
and frankly, not the way I wanted.
Unabashed love has a magnetic pull,
which attracted the energy I was releasing.
This perspective played tricks on my mind.

Despite what I thought I was feeling,
disappointment took center stage,
while love only made a guest appearance.
All the heartbreaks, the discouraging moments, the tears,
filled my heart, leaving no room for bliss.
I cracked repeatedly.

I won't defend the choices I made.
Decisions with a glimpse of hope, and a cloudy mind.
Not quite the components needed for the love I desired.
But, I chased it desperately,
exhausting my mind countless times
in trying to figure it out.

All that resulted was weariness.
I lost optimism, I lost hope.
The absent ingredient,
without which a toxic concoction brewed,
was to love myself.
It was that simple.

Today, the chase has finally concluded.
I realize love has always been there, and in ways I didn't see.
I don't need to run, there is no desire to control my future.
My energy can't be wasted in trying.
Appreciating living and being grateful fuels me.
Inspiration is at my center,
and the love I discovered has given me this endless gift.

Transformed

"There's a crack (or cracks) in everyone… that's how the light of God gets in."
~Elizabeth Gilbert

Having a stroke at age twenty-nine is both shocking and surreal. I was completely lost in my head, heart, and life. I began to develop a new appreciation of things I used to overlook, and started doubting all that I had trusted before the stroke. I looked for logic and reason to explain this collapse of my life. I felt that my past had somehow proven unworthy and so forced this transformation. The guilt tied to that thought left me drowning in an ocean of misery. For months, I was stuck in what and who to believe, how to rediscover normalcy, and how to regain awareness. One thing I did know was that there was a message I had to uncover.

My life was plagued with uncertainty and a level of grey that would not allow me to see color. I was exhausted by discomfort and indecision. Ghosts of the past visited me nightly. Situations where I had questioned my choices would wake me when I was lucky enough to sleep, and this all occurred while trying to figure out what to do about the very real hole in my heart.

My stroke was due to an 'Atrial Septal Defect' – or in layman's terms, a hole in my heart. The irony of the physical hole, which left me with an emotional hole, did not escape me. Hearts are divided into four chambers and the top-right section of the heart takes blood in and pushes it to the lungs. Lungs then work as a filter and push the blood to the top-left of the heart. That side is responsible for sending blood and oxygen to the entire body, including the brain. What happened to me is that this hole allowed a blood clot to go directly from the right side to the left. Then, it shot up straight to my brain, which was not able to get the oxygen, and resulted in the stroke.

The hole in my heart forced me to examine my life. First, my work environment was stressful and not especially conducive to good health. In addition, there were certain relationships around me that were not healthy. Because I was in a sort of purgatory on Planet Earth, I couldn't make sense of who, or what baggage, to rid myself of. But my undying optimism in the innate goodness of people took over my judgment to the point of fault. I couldn't assess whether I was doing the right thing, or if I was somehow being manipulated. This haze of confusion and doubt held me in this purgatory. All of the stresses took a toll on me mentally, physically, spiritually, and emotionally, during the most inopportune time in my life.

It's funny how you might think you know what you are doing at a certain point, achieve a little vision as to what to do, and pursue whatever you think will make you happy. Then, in an instant, it changes somehow, whether because of your own efforts, the emotions of others, or unforeseen circumstances. My life had been a series of intersections like this and I was tired of and frustrated by it. I recognized there is one thing that absolutely cannot be controlled – and that is your last day on earth.

Too much of my life had been spent on unnecessary moments, emotional dramas, and things lost in time. My life almost ended on February 22, so time became an invaluable commodity in my perspective. I didn't want to be so vulnerable to the environment I created anymore. The stroke took my confidence and shook my world, but gave me the impetus to change my life.

On June 1st 2009, I opted to have heart surgery to have the hole closed. This was the first step to regain order in my life. It's interesting: the first poem written four days before my stroke (or before my epiphany), titled "Losing Myself," specifically asked for a time out in life in order for me to reflect, regroup, and embrace the life I was blessed with. What better time than when the hole in my heart (and hopefully my head) was closed? Had I failed in my life, or had I learned and grown? I began to understand the importance of not repeating past mistakes and this insight was positive – just what my soul was searching for. I was on to something essential. I needed to flourish and resolved to not let go of this powerful perspective for anything, or anyone.

The following thoughts reflect my journey to let go and grow...

Who I Am

I can't comprehend the negativity you exposed me to.
How you broke my heart,
the tears you allowed me to shed,
how you caused me to lose my way.
You tormented my soul for so long.
I can still feel the tears stinging my eyes...
Through an era of darkness,
there were pockets of light.
Moments when I knew there was more
than what I was living,
and yet, you controlled me.
I entered environments that haunt me.
You used this to your advantage repeatedly.
But now, I know your games.
Your calculated ways are obvious.
Nothing about you merits respect.
The only good thing you brought to my life,
was knowledge of how 'not' to live.
I vow to everything of importance,
you will never have power over my spirit again.
I will guard it as a mother protects her child.
I will meet my potential.
There is no fear in acknowledging you were once in my life.
I am not scared of what others will think
about my experiences with you.
These are my stories, the scars I share with others,
to protect them from experiencing a sea of lies,
such as you brought to my life.
Wisdom I gained is not for me alone.
There is better than you in this world.
I am a soldier for a team of light.
My last breath will fight for this conviction to be evident,
and my life will reflect this truth.
Your perplexing ways, your path to nowhere…
it has ended with me.
You do not have this power over me.
In time, you will see who I am.

Nothing Can Hold Me Back Now

I had a powerful obsession.
It managed to confuse me.
Faithfulness, love, persistence presented themselves,
yet, something did not feel right.
I was influenced to attempt something I didn't *feel*.

During my time of confusion,
I couldn't decrypt which way was up, which down.
My mind was tormented during this breakdown.
All I thought I knew, was facade.
My foundation was broken, so much uncertainty.
I lived a private hell.
Memories, mistakes, and regrets of the past
inundated my mind.
I couldn't escape the depths of these pains,
though I inflicted most of my own agonies.
Moments I will live with the rest of my life
took form and grew from my poor choices.

The mirror forced me to look at the past,
and I realized this is not a legacy
I want to leave behind.
I have insight now, but still I am tested.
There have been tears and moments of loneliness.
The concrete around my soul had to be smashed,
in order for my spirit to become true and fly.
The years of bondage no longer encase my heart…
I can't survive in environs not meant for me.
I choose to change my surroundings.

My regrets of the past will turn to strength,
appreciation of the joys of life I am blessed with.
The power of words fills me with passion.
I am grateful to have a second chance for legacy.
No one can ever have power over my spirit again.
I desire nothing more than truth and love.
Love of family, friends, and love of self.
The intimacy within my heart cannot be substituted.
It can only grow from now.
Adversity is faced with the strength of my spirit.
And as many times as my growth was inhibited in the past,
nothing can hold me back now.

Forgive and Forget

'Forgive and forget' has entered my mind.
For years, I'd heard this is the best way to move on.
Countless times, I tried to forget wrongs I've encountered,
but all I achieved was avoidance.
I thought 'forget' meant to not talk about the incident,
pretend it didn't happen, move on.
But for years, these occurrences provoked memories,
some unforgotten as they lingered on inside of me.
I am forgiving, so why can't I forget?
With time, I learned a certain truth.
Forgiveness is an achievable part of life,
but 'forget' is not necessarily possible.

A result of the years I avoided,
the 'forget' incidents increased inside of me.
At times, thoughts were so strong they evoked tears.
Other times, I didn't know how
to face another day enduring the pain.
Could I possibly learn to perceive things differently now?
The answer is, yes.

My heart has learned 'forget' is not always possible.
And that 'forget' is multi-layered.
I've had to decide if it's worth carrying the pain.
Silence can no longer accompany 'forget.'
Ignoring the voice that haunted me,
only made it grow stronger.

Truth, words, and removing myself from the fear of others,
enabled me to be free from purgatory.
For those who have hurt me, I have hurt myself more
for carrying these pains in secret, in silence.
One by one, I face the reflections from my past and realize,
they are just that, passed.
Forgive is a struggle, something I will achieve.
Forget has occurred to an extent.
But I will always remember the importance of what happened.

Those memories protect me
from living with situations that don't belong in my life.
So have I learned 'forgive?' Absolutely.
Forget can be found in the sense that
you cannot change what has already occurred.
Most importantly, grow wiser with each experience.

Spread Thin

I have begun connecting the dots,
as I am faced with future options.
So many possibilities and dreams.
It has become loud in my mind and
I see clearly what needs to be done.
Every alternative,
could possibly leave a person behind.
The voices of these people are vivid,
yet, my heart encourages me to continue.
Should I explain, justify, what I am doing?
My actions surely are clear enough
for people not to judge.
I am doing my best to juggle it all,
but at the expense of my sanity.
There is no malice in my motives –
my desires stem from inspiration.
Will others see this truth?
All I know, is that I cannot break.

I won't be overwhelmed by what others may think.
The fire in my heart is distinct.
I have no goal to prove it.
A specific vision keeps me living passionately.
I am spread thin, of course, only human –
while these insights run deep.
I recognize my past may elicit doubt.
Nonetheless, I have to keep moving forward.
There are many roadblocks ahead on this journey.
My loved ones cannot become obstacles too.
This perspective is planned.
Focus is needed.
This fight may cause casualties,
I can only pray not to those I love.

Let Go

Sometimes in life, we come across pillars of the past.
Moments that molded us into who we are today.
Some essential pieces of our souls
are entangled with those memories
we'd rather forget.

But even those encounters play a crucial part,
in the puzzle of our lives.
What can be hard is when emotions
haunt and leave us vulnerable.
The complications, which sculpted an impression,
leave a mark on our hearts.

"Why does it still hurt so bad?"
I find myself asking after so many years.
The only truth I can assume,
is that all experiences penetrate the soul.
The most hurtful impressions, I have to accept.
I can't change, alter, or fix it. It just "is."

My heart has been touched,
as I struggle with these feelings.
The souls I love more than my life,
my team of encouragement,
understanding, and strength,
have blessed me by sharing their wisdom.

Common advice is to just 'let go.'
I can't change what occurred.
I may never truly understand motives behind the actions,
of those I loved – the ones who hurt me.
All I can do is love, let go, and grow.

Grow in compassion, grow in forgiveness –
even beyond my scope of understanding.
It's not easy,
I would be lying if I said it was simple.
But there is a bigger future awaiting.
My heart has to be ready for the next part,
and this can only occur when I truly let go.

Finding Peace

I try to contain the thoughts in my mind,
figure out what they mean... what should I write?
There are times I can't control the thoughts.
An internal voice is so powerful,
much deeper than I can comprehend.
It builds a level of curiosity that I'm compelled to pursue.
The energy inside of me is tenacious.
I was scared of it in the past.
I wasn't ready to understand its strength.
There were so many barriers holding me back,
situations thrusting me back to the beginning.
At times, the beginning was way ahead of me.

I ran tirelessly, determination present,
though my limited scope
tried to hold me back from internal strength.
Things were cloudy, my perception distorted.
At times night felt like day, day seemed to be night.
I lived with pain in my heart.

And now, I know what it would be like
to not wake up with the ability of 'change.'
Change everything I felt was wrong,
the injustices I lived amongst, lived in.

I realize my gift is my life.
All other things are disposable.
My core, where my joy resides, is simple.
It's love – love of family, friends, love in a genuine state.
A love I did not embrace in the past; love of myself.
I chose my surroundings.

The lack of my own conviction
that did not allow for the importance of
protecting my soul.
These scars are what shield me
from committing such mistakes,
as I protect this delicate,
but resilient, element of my being.
It's now filled with love,
purpose, a certain mindfulness.
This peace is what completes me.

A Woman's Story

As I look at myself, the curves of my body,
the texture of my hair,
the accent that colors certain expressions,
I wonder, what is my story?

The past has been full of experiences,
a range of emotions.
Many mysteries have evoked my curiosity.
Some situations will always have a shade of gray
that I may never understand.
There are certain circumstances I will never fully grasp.
Though the desire to understand,
brings a level of comfort to my being.

I hear the stories of my ancestors,
and like a child with a puzzle,
I begin to connect the pieces.
Until recently, I lived in a vacuum.
At the center was nothing other than me.
But now, my internal self wants to look back.
It wants to hear about the heritage,
the experiences the family lived through.
I want to bring back to life the memories of the past
in order to understand today.

As simple as such a physical aspect as,
"Why am I so curvy?"
A question that may be solved with a simple picture.
More important is the depth of my soul.
A soul that developed from those who came before me.
Though some I never met, their stories still affect mine.
And my life resulted from decisions they made.
A single different choice by any one of them,
could have altered the perfect chain of events,
which has me laying in my bed, writing now.

A "woman's story" is what I hope to learn,
and not just my own.
I seek the story that transcends culture, language, religion.
The story that evokes emotion,
and allows us to see how alike we are,
rather than how different.
I hope I'm lucky enough to capture the human spirit.
I pray for guidance and strength.
I hope my simple words are able to
express this amazing truth.

Understanding

As I look out of the window,
all I see is a blanket of white
covering the grass, trees, all of nature.
It is beautiful, simple, quiet, and honest.
There is a calm in the air.
A perfect mix for a night of memories.
It's ironic how these thoughts,
can resurface many emotions.
I can place myself back in situations,
and realize why I made certain decisions.
While there were times of happiness,
there were also distinct moments of pain.
This chain of events built the life I remember.
I read the words of the past,
and recognize I simply was not ready.
I wanted that special connection,
love is what I deeply yearned for,
but my mind did not understand
the magnitude of my true desires.
As I study my old journal pages,
I want to return to the past
and warn my younger self of
how certain decisions would alter my life.
But that is not how it works.
There was a specific purpose to it all.
I understand why things happened.
I am here, writing, and have focus.
This couldn't have occurred without each experience.
This series of events keeps unfolding day by day,
in its perfect order.
To think the word "perfect" belonged to my journey,
would have been, on occasion,
like adding salt to an open wound.
Yet, I am here today,
accepting the complex truth,
that everything does happen for a reason.
There was a plan,
I was being prepared for what is next.
The love I desperately searched for in the past,
is already here.

Alive

"The heart's memory eliminates the bad and magnifies the good; and thanks to this artifice we manage to endure the burdens of the past."
~Gabriel García Márquez

Now that my heart was physically closed, I knew my life was going to take a drastic turn, because my new heart was open at the same time. I had a deep appreciation for my life. While I healed physically, I had to heal my emotional heart and remove layers of the past and present that were still stressful and stagnant. I longed for clarity and understanding. Nothing, not even a hole in my heart, and nobody, not even my drained psyche, was going to stop me.

There were aspects of my life that I had the ability to change immediately. My return to work was on the table. I made a list of reasons to stay, versus reasons to leave. After seeing my words on paper, it wasn't even a decision anymore. Clearly, letting go to pursue my true, newly discovered, but ever-present purpose, was what I had to do. Life is too short to stay in an environment that swamped me in anxiety and stress. These elements were not part of the formula needed to reach my potential, my desires, and my destiny. So, I moved on.

Around the same time, I resolutely removed relationships in my life that weren't healthy. I had unwittingly allowed in people who manipulated love in an effort to keep me close. Those relationships were harmful to the metamorphosis I was going through, toxic even. Though love may have existed at some point, there was more strife, confusion, and stress in the equation, outweighing the love. I began to understand the dynamics of these individuals. I didn't see enough laughter, trust, or honesty. The relationships were damaging, and even though it was difficult, I had to let them go, regardless of how my memory romanticized them.

There was something beyond my physical self, something in the pit of my stomach, or maybe in the depths of my heart, that gave me strength. I didn't know where it was coming from or what it was; all I knew was I had to listen. I had to listen to my gut, to my heart. But this kind of listening meant patience, and I was not wired to possess patience as a natural virtue. I actively sought patience in order to gain real understanding and truth.

As human nature would have it, in the past I had bargained with myself; I compromised, and negotiated, looking for an easy way out, or for where I could have it all. However, this train of thought did not always align itself with truth or reality. I recognized that I am accountable for all decisions and relationships in my life, both good and bad, whether I like it or not.

The transformation was taking root, and I began to see life again. Once the seed of patience for my decisions, for my deepest needs, began to blossom, I chose to start living in a way I wanted to remember.

On August 29th, I finished reading an amazing memoir, *Paula*, by the brilliant writer Isabel Allende. The story resonated with my heart and mind; it was so powerful. Allende's ability to bare her soul during the darkest hour of her life, for the sake of inspiring others to help themselves, made me understand that I, too, had a purpose. In her book, certain stories spoke to my passion for helping others, and that connection gave life to the person inside of me who was waiting to come out.

As I finished the last page, I felt compelled to share how grateful I was for her beautiful gift of writing. Her words helped to inspire me to live the life for which I was destined. I wrote her an email with words of gratitude flowing from my heart. I appreciated her candidness and told her how I thought my own words might inspire others to pursue their destiny. She confirmed my conviction that I had the power to change myself and to inspire others to live their lives to the fullest. She also mailed an autographed book. Her generosity and selflessness to take time to respond to me was truly touching. She taught me that I would have the same obligation when my words touched others. Her spirit welcomed me to the world of writing. I smiled, cried, and danced about the connection we had made; it felt so right. Her selfless writing and response taught me a major lesson: sharing my goals, dreams, and healing, without fear, are essential in the pursuit of my dreams. On September 3rd, it hit me that I was on to something. How do I know all these dates you may be asking? It's because it was part of what I was on to. I was keeping a journal and writing everything and anything. The experiences I was living, the fear I felt, the appreciation, the uncertainty were all moments that needed to be captured on paper. It was therapeutic to release my thoughts from mind to paper. It was as if releasing these thoughts removed the possibility of it becoming something destructive internally. Silence was removed from the equation, and truth had the ability to really grow.

For the next couple of months, I attempted to identify what story was trying to take form in my mind. There were countless options from personal experiences and fictional stories that had potential to become a book. In the meantime, I organically wrote poems to help me get through the obstacles of that time.

In November of 2009, I took a memoir writing class in New York. I figured a memoir was the best medium to release the vision in my head. In this class, we were given writing exercises that pushed the mind to really think and find a focus to the story. One of the last exercises was to write concisely the point of your story. When I tried to do this simple task, I was stuck. I couldn't write, because I didn't know what story I wanted to share. Did I want to write about failed relationships, career disappointments, almost losing my life? At that time, I felt frustrated because I was confused. But this was the best thing that could have happened.

A few weeks after wrestling with, "What is the point of my memoir?" it hit me as I was driving on Tuesday, November 24th. I had been writing these poetic vignettes and there was a story connecting all these writings. You could see the personal struggles and desire of a person to grow. And the title hit me instantly. Butterflies had, and still have, such a significant role in my life, and I was writing my thoughts. So, that Tuesday, *Thoughts of a Butterfly* was born.

This is when I began to write my heart out. Things that made sense, things that didn't – whatever it was, it was being written. In addition to this power being unleashed, I recognized that, while it was an honorable goal to write, I hadn't the slightest idea of how to write a book. This is when I sought guidance and developed a level of discipline to learn the craft.

Writing became my best friend and I wanted her around all the time. The writing class, the books I was reading, and, most important, the support of family and genuine friends, opened up a new world for me. I felt blessed to have all these positive inspirations around me and realized that they were always there. The difference now was I was choosing this fundamental truth to be my center and guide on the new journey I was getting ready to embark on. My mind became a sponge, and all I wanted to do was absorb, absorb, absorb. I felt my life would change.

Time to spread my wings and fly...

A Mother's Love

As I look back at the scenes of my past,
I am lucky to see one constant link threading the story together.
I was blessed with the gift of a Mother's love.
Childhood memories circle in my mind,
as I recognize the message there to learn.
Like a timeless love story, the recurring picture,
no matter whether the story evoked happy or sad feelings,
my mother's comfort and warmth were always there
to accompany me through my journey.

For years, I overlooked her solid presence.
I took it for granted, assuming
she is 'Mom,' that is what she is supposed to do.
But now I know, she didn't *have* to do a thing.
There is a greater force, a love in her heart,
which has become completely evident to my soul and mind.
Her humility added compassion to my reasoning.
Her kindness softened the harsh realities I lived.
Her perspective gave me eyes to see another side of life.

I will never forget the strength and courage she has exuded,
at a time in our lives when we could have fallen apart.
The weight of the world fell on her gentle shoulders,
and without hesitation, she carried it all, as she saw something,
she tuned into something our blurred eyes could not see.
She held on tight and never spoke ill to cloud our minds.
If she felt pain, she carried it alone, only showing us love.
It was her conviction as a woman, a mother,
that meant class and dignity
were the characteristics to shine brilliantly
and adorn her broken heart.

I reflect how purpose and determination
always kept her focused.
There has always been a vision in her heart,
one that needs neither words, nor description.
It simply "is."
And to know her is to see it.
She is a woman of few words.
She is not showy, extravagant, or ostentatious.
Her ways don't require explanation.
There is something sincere about her spirit.
She radiates a timeless warmth.
One best described as,
to the fortune of my brother and I,
a mother's incredible love.

Fighting Spirit

Shirley, you need to get up…
"I can't… I just can't."
For hours, this sequence played in my mind.
Then it happened,
a jolt shocked my sleeping soul.
I felt something, though I did not understand what.
I couldn't make sense of where I was.
Thankfully, the sound was unmistakable,
I discerned a ring, and knew I *had* to wake up.
Determination led me,
love pushed through the barricades that tried to close me in.
Camaraderie was present in spirit that day.
A quilt of thoughts and prayers
kept me warm, as my body came closer to cold.
It was not my time.
I understand this clearly now.
Clouds cannot conceal this unequivocal truth.
The connection to these special souls,
who blessed my life in ways I am still discovering,
saved my life.
Their strength gave me fuel.
Words are not sufficient to express my gratitude.
I am blessed to share experiences with them.
For years, I overlooked their significance –
I did not bare witness to the depth of our connections.
I see now, they are the basis for the fighting spirit in my heart.
This realization changed my life.
Our connections guide and protect me on my journey.
However long or short it is, my experiences today plant seeds of love.
I pray this continues, long after I am gone.

Borrowed Time

Goodbye my loves, souls that blessed mine.
They guided my journey,
protecting me when I walked in the dark.
I will be eternally grateful for these bonds.
These spirits live in my heart,
distant memories live in my soul.
Some kind of wisdom materializes,
when I look back at my path –
as if they knew their purpose
and spoke words I recall vividly.
A bittersweet goodbye is all I can offer.
Borrowed time is what we exchanged.
I feel they knew before I did,
the path that needed to be paved.
I thank what I call my 'guardian angels.'
I hope to see them again,
and goodbye will never be traded.
Until I cross that bridge, I keep their fire going.
Their legacy lives within me.
As lucky as I have been to experience love in my life,
I must share this with others.
It will grow, flourish, become bountiful.
I feel compelled to make each day count.
Love must triumph, even in moments of wanting to give up.
This is a lesson for a lifetime,
and daily, this principle grows in strength.
Without my adjusting, it becomes what destiny desires –
and all this is happening on borrowed time.

What Follows Beauty

The gift of beauty is special, lovely.
It's nice to look in the mirror and like what you see,
but what you can't see should be inspected more closely.
I've learned that beauty brings a level of attention and charisma into life.
There are those who want you around,
simply for how your presence makes them feel.
It has taken me years to understand this.
I didn't want to realize people can be so shallow.
I did not understand the power physical beauty wields.
The saying, "Beauty is in the eye of the beholder" is true,
but it does not pay enough justice
to the notion of 'true' beauty.
There is more to a person than how they externally appear.
The dynamics of people alter,
when they focus on the wrong thing.
Beauty is inherently a good thing.
It's lamentable when some use it for manipulation.
This does not mean one shouldn't appreciate it, but,
also be aware motives sometimes have to be analyzed.
True beauty is within the heart –
thoughts, connections to others, the desire to simply be 'good.'
I see beauty today because
I love my family, I adore my friends… I'm grateful to be here.
Beauty is waking up in the morning,
knowing how lucky I am to share my life with those I love.
In my perspective, what follows beauty?
True love accompanies true beauty.

A Night in NYC

It's amazing how life can change in an instant.
I am sitting looking at a breathtaking view.
My heart contains a calm it hasn't had in years.
Words cannot do justice to describe
how grateful I am in all that surrounds me.
My mind is filled with inspiration – stories I want to share.
A certain level of love to be released.
A much stronger spirit now leads the way.

I am in my favorite city in the world.
The irony of this moment is that, a year ago,
as I first looked out on this view –
out of this window – and said, "I want this,"
"this" meant living in New York,
in a great apartment, with a spectacular view.
Not in a million years did I ever contemplate,
"this" referring to the inspiration I feel when I write.

I find beauty in places I overlooked in the past.
My desires and dreams
have a bigger purpose than my personal needs.
My wants have changed form,
transported to a stage much larger than my own.
A focus has taken over.
A shield that protects me from environments
that inspire nothing but chaos.
It can't happen again – I don't belong to confusion.
Love has found me and will not release me.
My eyes only see truth.
The truth of spirit, being, the gift of life.
This is my center, this is who I am.
My life will reflect appreciation,
because I am lucky to be here.

Voice in My Mind

I can remember my first encounter with my Spirit.
I was a little girl when it occurred.
Looking back, the innocence of childhood
taught me a lesson I recall today.
It was the first event in the long chain of stories,
which has assembled my life.
All the tales live in my mind.
At any moment, a memory can take me back.
What I've learned is when to purposely
evoke certain occurrences.
More importantly, how wisdom guides me to understand.
The gift is not to regret decisions of the past,
or to feel shame for things that didn't turn out right.
It's truly the gift of reflection, a chance to enhance perception.
The vision wasn't always clear.
For many years, I struggled to grasp this concept.

There were days I lived in perfect calm,
but so quickly, the tides could transform.
The sea of my life changing shape,
volatile waves submerging all in their way.
Sadly, at the expense of my being.
But with time, steps to the next level illuminate.
A certain intuition protects me.
There is a fire beneath this motion –
a passion unleashed, with distinct purpose.
Negativity will always exist, but now I see past it.
My vision passes through the images of fear,
sadness, confusion…
My heart knows what message to listen for.
Confidence in this belief solidifies daily.
This is the voice in my mind.

A Change in Perspective

It's been an amazing day,
inspiration taking center stage.
I can't begin to explain what I saw,
all I can say is,
there has been a change of heart.
The energy I felt today
was out there waiting for me.
I have engaged with a special connection.
A remarkable interdependence emerged.
It took a little more than luck to 'get' it.
I couldn't *see* a power unmeant for human eyes.
Rather, I believed in a feeling designed for the soul.
It was always there, just overlooked in years past.
A simple change in perspective,
bestowed this grace upon me today.
I want to share this gift with the world.
Open your eyes, and prepare your heart.
Believe in something bigger than you.
It's out there for all of us.
This doesn't mean every day will be wonderful.
Bliss mustn't be confused with selfish desires.
There is a brilliance in our world,
one we are meant to meet.
It strengthens our foundations,
so, don't be scared of the unknown.
Explore, be curious, yet aware.
Let go of the negative thoughts,
laugh instead of cry, begin to really live,
and let love guide your heart.

One Day

As I look back and contemplate the past,
the sequence of events –
tears, laughter, confusion, and the love…
Finally, it has all come together.
In years past, I did not see it.
Days were lost in ambivalence.
Today, though, it all makes sense.
There was method in the way things occurred.
In the moments of despair, this vision was not evident, but
hope was always present, even in the dark.
A simple desire for better days did not dwindle away,
though at points, my dream was far from realization.
All the lessons from childhood,
the phrases from those older, wiser than me,
advice to protect on my journey.
The words I thought didn't make sense,
words I thought I was too good for,
I see their flow today, how they relate to life.

It is here.
The dream, love, and hope I couldn't have imagined.
It has weaved unparalleled perception.
A grace now guides this path.
There is no reason to ask, "Why now?"
A level of comfort has warmed my heart
and I appreciate it.
All I can say, with humility, is, "Thank you."
Life will continue to evolve
with many future bridges to cross.
Obstacles will undoubtedly impede the way,
but a special connection will always be there
to guide… I just have to listen.
It is amazing to think, this bond was always there,
waiting for me to recognize it.
One day it came together –
I saw it, and now I know.

Ready

"There are only two ways to live your life. One is as though nothing is a miracle.
The other is as though everything is a miracle."
~Albert Einstein

By this point you may be wondering, "What's up with the butterfly?" Of course, there is a story behind this inspirational force.

On April 29th, 2000, a difficult experience left me questioning the truth of life and my purpose. On April 30th, while I cried torrential tears I never knew were possible, I was compelled to return to my roots and found myself back at my high school. There, with uncertainty about my life, I questioned why I had been exposed to such anguish. In a moment of despair, I asked God, "Do you even exist?"

As I walked around the track, I began to talk to God. I desperately needed, and asked for, a sign to let me know somehow that this mess would be okay one day. The heavens did not open up and rain their wisdom, patience, or empathy upon me. What did happen was a butterfly fluttered next to the left side of my face. It lingered close enough that I could feel the wind from its tiny wings. My only thought was, "Is that really a butterfly flying so close to my head?"

It was there for at least thirty seconds – just enough time for my feelings to turn from shock, to a deep appreciation that my prayer had been answered. It was my sign, and once I recognized the depth of what had occurred, the butterfly took a sharp right turn, brushed against my nose, and flew up in the air. It's been eleven years since I lived this story, and each time I think about it, my understanding of the significance of what occurred deepens.

The experience left an impression on my being. It showed me I will never be alone. The past eleven years, a butterfly seems to come out of nowhere when I need a "sign," or confirmation of what to do. There has always been an energy that protected me, even while in an emotionally distressed state. With time, this energy has strengthened, especially when I lost the fear of vocalizing its existence. The butterfly has now transformed from a beautiful insect to an instinctive power that guides me. Even though she now lives inside me, I do still like seeing her. It makes me smile.

Two years ago, when I suffered my stroke at age 29, was categorically the event that reshaped my life. There have been many unexpected encounters since the stroke that sparked my desire to make change. The most important was the fact that I had a stroke on my brother's birthday. That wasn't coincidental; there was a purpose to it and my awakening occurred that day. Since then, I've managed to break past behaviors and rewire my brain to create the internal change to live life differently. This change has not been simple to say the least. It's not as though I had an epiphany and boom, all of a sudden everything was perfect. It hasn't been an easy journey, but what could I expect? I had accumulated a lot of baggage through the years – unloading it was not going to be simple.

My mind and heart had to become one and develop a level of trust I did not possess in the past. The separation of mind and heart was a big part of the reason I suffered so much. Although I recognize this, it doesn't mean life becomes easy. That is not how it works. What I've been lucky to achieve is an understanding and acceptance that all things happen for a reason. There were certain lessons I had to learn, and through them, I gained experience, which has now evolved to wisdom. For me, the most important aspect of this growth has been to distance myself from unhealthy situations such as bad relationships, destructive surroundings, energy thieves, and anything tied to negative energy. I can't avoid all negative or unproductive aspects of life (I would have to live in a bubble to achieve this). However, I have chosen to be mindful and aware of my surroundings. Though I come across negativity, I choose not to engage.

One night, while hanging out with my brother and friends, I had a powerful thought. Observing our interactions that night; the laughter, the story-telling, being forthcoming with fears and just living, I came up with what I now call my "Four L's." It has become something of a motto for me – how I hope to live my life.

First, in life, many things happen to us all. The emotional spectrum that molds our lives exposes us to occurrences we need, in order for our character to take shape. Sometimes these experiences are troubling and we may question why we are living with such grievances. Here is where my first "L" can help: Let go. There is nothing we can do to change our past, or to create an environment tweaked to best fit us. There is so much we can't control, and when we accept this and realize there is a plan in it all, somehow it becomes a little easier. Sometimes we are not meant to 'get it' right away, so letting go of control, instead of forcing an issue, can actually help achieve a better life. It's damaging to try to dictate every part of life.

My second "L" is: Laugh. The same night with my brother and friends clearly demonstrated the importance of laughter and what a gift it truly is. To find humor in our fearful circumstances can lessen the impact of the situation. This in turn can bring a level of calmness, which may result in a brighter outcome, or conscious acceptance. Being able to laugh at yourself means you do not take yourself too seriously. If that isn't enough to inspire you, laughter is better than sorrow. Tears cannot be erased from the equation – they are part of life. But laughing is too, and it's something we can choose to experience.

The third "L" is to: Live. Maybe things are not one hundred percent how you want; your job sucks, you are not personally where you want to be, you don't know where you want to be, etc. This is all okay and quite normal. Nevertheless, in the moments of question, and the many crossroads we all experience, living is key to releasing the outcome you are meant to experience. Wake up and be grateful for just "getting up." When walking outside, look at the trees, the sky, flowers, birds, even the guy spitting on the streets of New York! Really look at all the beauty that surrounds you daily and appreciate your ability to see. If you are walking, thinking, or have the capacity to do, then you are lucky. That in itself is a blessing, and living with this knowledge promotes a sense of gratitude and appreciation.

Lastly, the fourth and most important "L" is: Love. Nothing great comes without love. Love surrounds us all the time, whether it is in nature, friends, or family. Love everything you do, even the things you think you don't like. I know that may sound odd, but truly seek to understand why you hate or dislike, and maybe it's a perspective you can choose to change within yourself. You will grow, evolve, and may become wiser. Love is our center; we were made to love, share love – and to live by this can change your life, and maybe the lives of those around you.

So there you have it, my four L's: Let Go, Laugh, Live, and Love... they now belong to you!

This leads me to today. I am now thirty-two years old and lived through a near-death experience. I am grateful for the stroke I suffered; it changed my life. This is the beginning of a new journey for me, and I want to share my experiences in hope of helping others who may be experiencing what I too felt; confusion, uncertainty, and lack of direction. My writings are my personal thoughts and revelations based on my life experiences. Understanding about several episodes that hurt my core has allowed me to bring closure to events of my past, and a level of peace into my heart that keeps me moving forward.

A friend of mine gave me some great advice as I embarked on this second chance of life. She said there would be many crossroads ahead, and usually the forks in the road offer two choices. One may be slightly easier and my patterns of the past could easily re-emerge with this choice. If I choose this path, I may feel fine for a short time, but it would be similar to using a band-aid on a wound that requires stitches. The healing process will leave a scar. The other option might be more difficult initially, because it would push me out of my comfort zone. Faith is essential with this choice, because the actions needed to get through the situation could feel foreign to me. It may be harder in the beginning, but taking this more difficult choice will not scar my spirit. Also, as time goes on, the strength and resilience that grows inside of me will make my decision at the next crossroad clearer to see. I thank my friend for her wise words.

To sum it all up, what I've learned is: If change is what I aspire to, I must look within my heart, listen for the voice that guides me, and listen. Looking deeply at what is going on, and confirming that love is at the center will help with direction. Most things in life are a process, and I've learned to be open to it whether it happens in days, weeks, months, or even years. Regardless of how long it takes, there is always something to learn. Sometimes the greatest insights are revealed during the process, thus patience helps along the journey, until the sweet moment of reaching the destination, wherever that may be.

This is where I am today. I have taken these steps, and push myself to keep growing and evolving as a person. I finally learned to really love myself, and, from experience, when you do this you can start to grow into the person God intended you to be… and here life gets interesting! I don't know what the future holds – there are no guarantees in life – but I do know I am lucky to be here today. It's that simple.

I hope my "thoughts of a butterfly" plant a seed of inspiration in your thoughts today, and always.

Thoughts of a Butterfly

It all began so long ago,
and yet, it seems like it just occurred.
A voyage of moments,
intersections of choices, decisions, consequences,
happened immaculately.
A certain truth accompanied this story.
A level of faith in something profound.
A vision only my heart could see.
No words can truly explain this life-altering phenomenon,
however, it's simple.
My mind is ready for the vision.

I want to live a life worth remembering.
The blinders are gone.
Love is present.
Wisdom, courage, faith, and belief closely follow.
Lessons and experiences opened my senses.
The cocoon I lived in, ready to be shed away.
I often go back to a specific memory,
one that was my crossroad.
That night, "I can't" was the only thought in my mind.
But here I am now,
fueled with fire, an energy.
I write, feel, and love – fear cannot contain this Spirit.
My mantra is, "You have to."
I don't know how long my journey will be.
There are moments, mysteries, and miracles I will live.
Thankfully, my heart is sound.
And today, in my mind,
are the Thoughts of a Butterfly.

For more information on stroke awareness, please visit:

www.stroke.org

www.strokeassociation.org

Special Thanks

Andrea Gagne
Cerian Griffiths
Alice McKenna
Adrian Muys
Laura Noselli
Roberto Carlos Perez

Creative Direction and Book Design
Bryan Ramos
www.zatorispark.com

Fine Art
Nena Depaz
www.geminigallery.com

Photography – About the Author
Peter Stepanek
www.skyhighart.com

Photography – Poems
Shirley J. Ramos

About the Author

Shirley J. Ramos was born on March 29, 1979, in Queens, New York. The daughter of immigrant parents from Colombia, South America, she is a first generation North American. Growing up amidst cultural diversity in Silver Spring, MD, varied influences helped shape Shirley's early outlook on life. She has an overall deep consideration for people, regardless of their background or circumstance.

Shirley's passion and purpose is focused on the assistance and inspiration of others. *Thoughts of a Butterfly* is the facilitation of that purpose. Surviving the near-death experience of a stroke at a young age transformed Shirley's perspective. It is this unique perspective that Shirley now hopes to share with others.

Thank you for reading *Thoughts of a Butterfly*.

Now it's your turn to capture a thought.

Title: _____

Date: _____

_____

_____

_____

_____

_____

_____

_____

_____

_____

_____

_____

_____

_____

_____

_____

_____

_____

_____

_____

_____

_____

_____

_____

_____

_____

_____

Would you like to share your thought with the TOAB community?

If so, please email your thought to:

community@toabutterfly.com

With your permission, we'll post your thought on TOAB's website.

Thanks!

Made in United States
North Haven, CT
12 September 2023

41452483R00062